Masterpieces
of
Italian Art

Maria Laura Della Croce

WHITE STAR
PUBLISHERS

CONTENTS

Text
Maria Laura Della Croce

Editorial Supervision
Valeria Manferto

Graphics
Patrizia Balocco

Editorial team
Fabio Bourbon, Anna
Galliani, Gianna Manferto

English translation editor
Irene Cumming Kleeberg

**English edition
production editor**
Leslie Bockol

First published by Edizioni White Star.
Title of the original edition:
Capolavoro Italia
World copyright © 1992 by Edizioni
White Star.

Printed in Italy by Pozzogros Monti,
Turin, Italy

ISBN: 0-7666-0123-4

Page 1
Turin, Church of St. Lorenzo,
Guarino Guarini, 1667-80

Pages 2-3
Michelangelo, Pietà, *1497-*
1500, Vatican City, St. Peter's
Basilica

Pages 4-5
Sandro Botticelli, Primavera,
1478, panel, Florence, Uffizi

Pages 6-7
Gianlorenzo Bernini, Apollo
and Daphne, *detail, marble,*
1622-25, Rome, Borghese
Gallery

Pages 8-9
Michelangelo, David, *marble,*
1501-04, Florence, Accademia

Pages 10-11
Ravenna, mausoleum of Galla
Placidia, fifth century

Pages 12-13
St. Peter's Basilica, Vatican
City, interior of the dome

Pages 14-15
Michelangelo, Sistine Chapel,
detail of the vault, 1508-12,
fresco, Vatican City

Page 17
Gianlorenzo Bernini, Rape of
Prosperine, *detail, 1621-22,*
marble, Rome, Borghese
Gallery

Pages 18-19
Pisa, Piazza dei Miracoli,
view with the Cathedral, the
deep apse, and the tower,
eleventh and twelfth centuries

Pages 20-21
Orvieto, cathedral, detail of
the decoration of the façade

INTRODUCTION

Italy, an immense treasure chest of precious objects of all kinds, has been described as an open air museum. This book shows this quality through a journey over the entire Italian peninsula. We will look at churches, squares, public and private buildings, and paintings, with particular attention to the role played by artists and craftsmen. We will investigate the ways in which they reflected the moods of their times while creating their own visions of that special world known as Italy.

The pictures in this book are stunning; for us, living in the present, they evoke emotions that were created in the past.

Centuries-old churches and cathedrals, cloisters and monasteries, squares created hundreds of years ago but still filled with activity, and palaces that reflect the lives lived in them . . . they speak to us today in much the same voices as in the past. Indeed, they speak for themselves. However, each chapter begins with a text. This is intended not as a critical analysis but rather as an accompaniment to the pictures — an explanation of juxtapositions, the development of new tastes, and changes in taste.

All that is needed to fully enjoy this book, then, is to leaf through the pages, pausing now and then to thoroughly study a particular photograph. Each page is, in and of itself, a work of art combining beauty with philosophy and, often, religion.

Maria Laura Della Croce

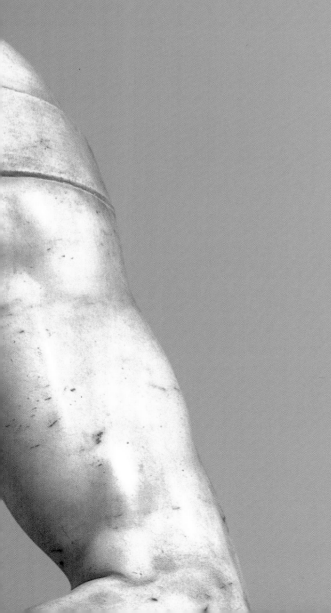

A GENIUS
FOR PORTRAITURE

A GENIUS FOR PORTRAITURE

Pages 22-23
Michelangelo, Moses, 1515,
Rome, San Pietro in Vincoli

Page 25
Masaccio, Crucifixion, 1426,
Naples, Capodimonte
Museum

One of the most outstanding elements shared by the majority of the pictures in this chapter is the great importance the artists attached to accurate portrayal of the human form. In both their religious and secular portraits, these artists show a vast range of feelings and emotions.

In addition, the artists used various symbols and physical attributes to send particular philosophical, theological, and moral messages to the viewer. Each work of art's original audience was familiar with this "code." The way in which the subject of the portrait is dressed, his clothing, hair style, the way he holds himself, the way he occupies the space of the portrait . . . today, these clues give us information about the history and tradition of the society to which he belonged.

The eighteenth-century French writer Stendahl, writing in his history of Italian painting, pointed out that different painters would paint the same subject quite differently. For example, the Adoration of the Magi: Michelangelo, he said, would show strength and awe; Raphael would stress the purity of Mary and the child; while Leonardo da Vinci would emphasize the nobility of the kings. Leonardo da Vinci's somber colors would have a somewhat depressing effect; on the other hand, Correggio would paint an amazingly rich feast for the eyes.

Stendahl also suggested that the twenty or thirty great painters would all have used different means to achieve their goals. The colors chosen, the ways of applying them, the use of light and shade, and certain accessories would all be part of the work. He pointed out, almost ironically, that a woman does not wear the same hat when she is meeting her lover as she does when she is going to confession; similarly, each artist brings to the subject matter his own view of society and reflects the role he played in it.

For centuries, artists considered themselves to be no more than somewhat refined craftsmen. Through at least the first half of the fifteenth century, they were modest people living modest lives, with neither their background nor their education separating them from the ordinary craftsman. Andrea del Castagno was the son of a farmer, Paolo Uccello of a barber, Filippo Lippi of a butcher, and the Pollaiolo brothers were the sons of a poultry seller. Giorgio Vasari, the great biographer of Italian artists, reports that Filippo Lippi couldn't afford a pair of socks; Paolo Uccello, when he was old, not only had no possessions, but also could no longer work and had an ill wife.

Viewed in this light, the great masters were workmen, following orders from a buyer, or religious conventions, or political necessities. For centuries these artists were asked to represent Divine Glory or the power and prestige of the Empire, and they did so.

With Giotto, at the beginning of the fourteenth century, the position of the artist began to make a slow change. Artists began to exercise an influence on contemporary culture while also interpreting this culture.

The Gothic period saw similarly complex changes. As great cathedrals were built in the name of God, there was a simultaneous movement toward humanization in sculpture — an abandonment of the solemnity and static nature of previous centuries' artwork. Freedom, great diversity of movement, more expression, richness, and variety in detail all appear in this period.

A comparison of the many statues in the Or San

Page 26
Donatello, David, c. 1430,
bronze, Florence, Bargello
Museum

The David, which Donatello
sculpted for Cosimo de'
Medici around 1430, is based
on the classical concept of a
naturally sized nude statue.
Although referring back to
Greek models, the sculptor
nonetheless brought his own
original interpretation to this
work. This David has almost
the air of a street urchin
beneath his comic head
covering. He combines a
victorious figure with
something of a painful and
restless adolescence, revealed
by his ambiguous smile.

Michele (commissioned by the guilds of craftsmen that led Florence's economic prosperity at the end of the fourteenth and beginning of the fifteenth centuries) shows this development clearly. For fifteen years, artists including Lorenzo Ghiberti, Nanni di Banco, and Donatello worked on this monument side by side, each bringing his own special talents to the work.

During the Renaissance, a man-centered view of the universe evolved. Artists moved to the forefront of civic life because they were the first to express fully the new aims which were becoming part of the cultural and political climate of Florence. The impact of the work of these artists was much stronger than any written manifesto could have been.

Stendahl pointed out that public demand for statues produced such artists as Donatello, Brunelleschi, Ghiberti, Filarete, Rossellino, Pollaiolo, and Verrocchio. They worked in a variety of materials, including marble, bronze, and silver, and their works were displayed throughout Florence. The artists' fellow citizens were greatly impressed, believing the works to equal the masterpieces of antiquity, although at that time no statues dating from the classical period had been found.

The discovery of perspective was formulated by Filippo Brunelleschi and discussed by Leon Battista Alberti in his "Trattato della Pittura" of 1436. Perspective is much more than just a skill and a technique for showing space. It is both a science and a relationship to reality which gives not only the artist but also the viewer access to a harmonious space with proportional relationships that faithfully reflect reality. Because the mechanical arts had both theoretical and scientific foundations, they gained new dignity and became part of the so-called liberal arts, thereby raising the prestige of the artists.

With the individualistic and practical development of the Florentine bourgeoisie, references to the classical world increased and a high regard for the individual and for creative activity developed. This led, albeit slowly, to a view of the artist as intellectual rather than as almost a manual laborer. Considering this, the tendency of artists to insert self-portraits into their paintings can be viewed as the artistic equivalent of the new autobiographical genre, first introduced by Lorenzo Ghiberti. Starting in the fifteenth century, the portrait developed its own autonomy, linked to the new importance of the individual. This was a major change from the Middle Ages, when portraits were almost always part of larger compositions.

This is especially true of the portrait bust, so characteristic of Roman times, which once again became extremely important. The fifteenth-century version was secular, and (like its Roman antecedents) reflected a desire to display the civic virtues of the person portrayed. The two major styles were vivid realism and idealization. For a long period idealization was to dominate; it became one of the most evident hallmarks of the new taste and of Renaissance culture.

During the sixteenth century, art reflected the contemporary view that self-control was the most desirable feature of a personality. Thus emotions, which in the fifteenth century had remained as relics of the late Gothic period, disappeared from art and portrait painting. Mary without tears or gestures views her dead son, just as in pictures of her with the baby Jesus all plebeian emotion is repressed. Balance is, in everything, of major importance; order and discipline in art reflected the sobriety and restraint of sixteenth-century life. The ideal was a sublime regularity, calm, and stability, in life as in art.

The concept of beauty is dependent on the human ideal of the aristocracy, with beauty and physical strength as the expression of spiritual value. The sibyls and Madonnas of Michelangelo show a gigantic, confident, and proud humanity expressing tremendous energy. The human ideal, presented by Baldassarre Castiglione in his book discussing ideal behavior in courtly circles, had tremendous influence not only in Italy and other countries on the Continent but as far away as the English court. He expressed these ideals as being not only attainable but often, indeed, as already attained. It was this ideal that is taken here as an example. The courtly ideal itself has all the essential characteristics of the image of man which sixteenth-century art gives us. Castiglione demanded from the perfect man of the world versatility, balanced development of physical and intellectual gifts, ease in the use of arms and in society, experience of poetry and music, and familiarity with painting and science.

The beauty and nobility of sixteenth-century heroic figures reflect in their images this human and social ideal. This style, strongly influenced by antiquity and often referred to as neoclassicism, is exemplified by such artists as Raphael and Michelangelo. It is also reflected in the ease of the figures' movements as well as in their relaxed and calm poses.

It was perhaps inevitable that there was a reaction to the neoclassical period. Following Raphael, who died in 1520, a new style emerged which is now called Mannerism. Its proponents — Pontormo, Parmigian-ino, Bronzino, Beccafumi, Rosso Fiorentino and Tintoretto — broke with the simple regularity and harmony of classical art and replaced its universality with more subjective and emotional characteristics. This rejection of classical forms manifested itself in many different ways, including a new spiritualism, a new intellectualism which deliberately deformed reality (often in favor of the bizarre), and a newly refined taste which rendered everything in terms of subtlety, acuteness, and elegance. This view of life granted new and previously unheard-of importance to dreams, which take real connections and turn them into abstract relationships between objects; taken to an extreme, this focus on dreams verges on the Baroque. In fact, Mannerism and near-Baroque style meet in some of the works of Raphael and Michelangelo, in which passionate Baroque expressionism meets with the intellectualism of Manneristic art.

The true character of Baroque is to expand the limits of reality, intensifying it in a thousand different ways, each more surprising, triumphant, and joyful than the previous one. The fashion of painted ceilings — gigantic optical illusions which inspire a particular type of dizziness — is, perhaps, one of the most impressive examples. Monumental sculpture also developed more creatively, thanks to such skilled portraitists as Gianlorenzo Bernini, who was highly gifted in conveying his own religious feelings of ecstasy and mysticism to others. Even his treatment of draperies was new, serving to accent the dynamic and dramatic effect of his work.

Painting is part of mankind's wish to "put the world on stage." To this end, it began to invent different trends and artistic schools, such as still life, land-

scape, and traditional domestic scenes. In the seventeenth century, each of these schools became isolated from the others, pushing artists to specialize in one or another of these genres: there were painters of flowers, ruins, musical instruments, battles, and so on. (The setting of scenes in a somewhat disjointed manner or from a diagonal viewpoint was also popularized at this time but it had less significance.)

For seventeenth-century critics, Caravaggio sheds great light on genre painting, particularly that of still lifes. He himself said that there was no difference between a painting of fruit and a painting of people. Caravaggio also brought to art a new and courageous way of painting light. The most important thing in his pictures is the presence of bodies, the solid and detailed reality of the object. His poetic originality lies in the way he used the maximum contrast of light and shadow; parts of his figures are drowned in darkness, from which a face, an arm, or a hand emerges in surprising relief. It has been said that Caravaggio's greatness lay in his ability to help us realize the dark side of the world and to surprise us with light and moving forms.

Sculptors also gave themselves over to this movement, learning from Bernini how to use a light whose source cannot be seen by the spectator. In contrast with the clear and diffused light of Renaissance artists, directional light seems transitory, giving spectators the feeling that the scene itself is transient. The light of Bernini is distinctly warm — and revolutionary.

But the cold and classic light of Antonio Canova shows a return to the basic beauty of early sixteenth-century classicism, inspired itself by classical antiqui-

Pages 30-31
Caravaggio, Supper at
Emmaus, *1606, canvas,*
Milan, Brera Art Gallery

ty. Canova's sculpture is the main Italian example of the rediscovery of classicism, which would become one of the bases of neoclassical art.

Canova presents in his work the image of both an intellectual and sublime grace, in which cold light has both metaphysical and symbolic meaning. Such coldness was seen by hostile critics as overly artificial, affected, and impersonal. Even today there are critics who feel the marble sculptures of Canova are smooth and cold (and, incidentally, erotic). Canova, however, took seriously a suggestion made by the major theoretician of the period, Johann Joachim Winckelmann — a suggestion that a return to classicism was necessary, and that strong emotions should play a part in art.

Canova's terra-cotta models have an immediacy, spontaneity and vitality which is extremely vivid. They have been cited more than once as proof that there was more than one side to Canova, a man who so loved the classics that he had the works of ancient writers read to him while he worked. It is said that Canova never tired of polishing and cleaning his works, attempting to give the marble a softer appearance by staining the statues with soot after polishing them to a high gloss.

The great artists of this era were so gifted that at times they created images more real than reality itself. Even their biographies point out their distance from ordinary life. Anecdotes are told of Caravaggio's quarrelsome and scandal-prone nature, the bizarre behavior of Pontormo, the fear that Michelangelo could inspire, da Vinci's dabblings in the occult, and Raphael's melancholy attacks. Little has changed in the modern world; even today opinion tends to recognize artists as extraordinary beings whose temperament and habits differ greatly from those of ordinary people. Artists are forgiven for many forms of extravagant behavior, for which other people would be condemned.

It should be noted that works of art have often been believed to have magical powers in and of themselves. During the Renaissance period, statues of bronze and wax were actually made for magical purposes. There is widespread belief that a strong connection exists between a painted or sculpted representation of a person and the person himself. This is the basis for one form of black magic, in which an image is damaged with the intent that the pain will be felt in the portrayed individual.

Of course, this belief is reciprocal — there is widespread belief that the damage that occurs to a person will be reflected in his portrait, as in Oscar Wilde's tale of Dorian Gray. Despite the continuing secularization of art, there is a human tendency to identify it with magic — and, in certain circles, to view the producer of these images as a magician. In Italy it is possible to identify with all of these many facets of art.

Page 34
Simone Martini,
Annunciation, 1333, central
part of the multi-paneled
work, panel, Florence, Uffizi

This is the last dated work
made by the Sienese painter
Martini before he moved to
Avignon. In this painting, he
expresses his own idea of
spiritual beauty not only in
the figures but also in the
objects, the fabrics, and the
flowers. His technique adds
elegance to the line and a
veritable glow to the images.

Page 35
Duccio da Buoninsegna,
Rucellai Madonna, 1285,
Florence, Uffizi

Pages 36-37
Duccio da Buoninsegna,
Maestà, *multi-paneled work,
back of the main panel,
divided into fourteen panels in
two rows. Siena, Museo dell'
Opera del Duomo*

Pages 38-39
Duccio da Buoninsegna,
Maestà, *detail*

*Page 40 left
Andrea Verrochio, La Dama
col Mazzolino, (Woman
with a Nosegay), 1475-
1480, marble, Florence,
Bargello Museum*

*The Florentine artist
Verrochio was originally a
goldsmith. His training as a
craftsman and his vast
experience both in drawing
and in the execution of chased
work is evident in his delicate,
smooth, graceful sculptures.*

*Page 40 right
Francesco Laurana, Bust of
Battista Sforza, c. 1472,
marble, Florence, Bargello
Museum*

*Page 41
Verrocchio, La Dama col
Mazzolino (Woman with a
Nosegay), detail*

*Francesco Laurana was a
Dalmatian artist who worked
in both Sicily and Naples. In
Naples he worked at the court
of Alfonso of Aragon. For
Federigo da Montefeltro, Duke
of Urbino, he produced this
portrait bust of the Duke's
wife, Battista Sforza, which
shows an almost geometrical
purity of form.*

Page 42
Benevenuto Cellini, Bust of
Cosimo I, *detail, 1545-48,
bronze, Florence, Bargello
Museum*

*This is an idealized portrait,
superbly produced by the most
fashionable artist of the day
for a great patron of the arts,
the Prince and Lord of
Florence. By this time
Florence was the capital of a
modern state.*

Page 43
Antonio del Pollaiolo,
Hercules and Antaeus, *c.
1475, bronze, Florence,
Bargello Museum*

*Pollaiolo, like Verrocchio, was
a goldsmith who also painted
and sculpted. He preferred to
model small bronzes rather
than larger sculptures. In this
work, light and shadow play
against each other to animate
the sculpture.*

A Dominican friar and member of the Order of Preachers, Fra Angelico was a strongly religious artist whose work provides an intense and fascinating insight into monastic life in the fifteenth century. His frescoes were painted in the cells and corridors of the San Marco monastery which was rebuilt

at Cosimo de' Medici's expense. The frescoes were designed to provide the monks with subjects on which to meditate. Quite often a Dominican saint is included as an example and inspiration.

*Page 44
Giovanni da Fiesole, known as Fra Angelico,* Crucifixion and Saints, *after 1438, from the frescoes in St. Mark's convent, Florence, chapter house*

Page 45 top
Fra Angelico,
Transfiguration of Christ,
cell 6 of the monastery
dormitory

Page 45 bottom
Fra Angelico, Adoration of
the Magi, *cell 39*

Pages 46-47
Fra Angelico, Crucifixion,
detail

This painting was commissioned by Cosimo de' Medici to commemorate the victory of the Florentines over Siena at San Romano in 1432. Although not actually historically correct, it was used by Paolo Uccello to show his own taste for the dramatic and perhaps a degree of skepticism. The event it depicted was soon forgotten, and the three panels which make up the scene were later often described simply as "jousts" or "tourneys."

THE WORK
OF PIERO DELLA
FRANCESCA

Page 50
Piero della Francesca,
Portrait of Battista Sforza,
c. 1465, Florence, Uffizi

Page 51
Piero della Francesca,
Portrait of Federigo da
Montefeltro, c. 1465, panel,
Florence, Uffizi

This pair of portraits of the Duke and Duchess of Urbino shows a strong taste for the meticulous detailing found in Flemish portraits. Piero della Francesca was an expert mathematician and the author of a basic treatise on perspective; here, he manages to paint the distant village in proportion with the irregularities of the Duke's very realistic profile, which includes curls, warts, and wrinkles.

Page 52
Piero della Francesca,
The Adoration of the True
Cross, *1459-62, detail from
the frescoes of* The Legend of
the True Cross *in the Church
of San Francesco, Arezzo*

*Here Piero's somewhat solemn
art is directed toward the
balanced, coherent, and
austere rendering of figures,
objects, and architecture. Each
form is a regular geometric
solid. Note the round heads
and the columnar necks, all
molded by very bright light.
After Piero became blind, he
dedicated his life to
mathematical speculation.*

Page 53
Piero della Francesca,
The Dream of Constantine,
1452-59, from the frescoes in
the church of San Francesco in
Arezzo

The ray of light which shines
from the angel and hits the
cone-shaped tent is one of the
first nocturnal views in the
history of fifteenth-century
painting.

Pages 54-55
Piero della Francesca, frescoes
in the church of San
Francesco, Arezzo, detail with
the Queen of Sheba

THE ARRIVAL OF LEONARDO DA VINCI

This poignant Pietà by Giovanni Bellini reveals a sad intimacy, both in the juxtaposition of the faces of the mother and child and in the clasp of their hands against the dark light of the background. Giovanni Bellini, the son of Jacopo, was the brother of Gentile (official portraitist of the Doges and brother-in-law of Andrea Mantegna).

Page 58
Giovanni Bellini, Pietà, 1460, panel, Milan, Brera Art Gallery

Page 59
Christ Against the Column, *1480-1490, tempera on panel, Milan, Brera Art Gallery*

Pages 60-61
Giovanni Bellini, Pietà, detail

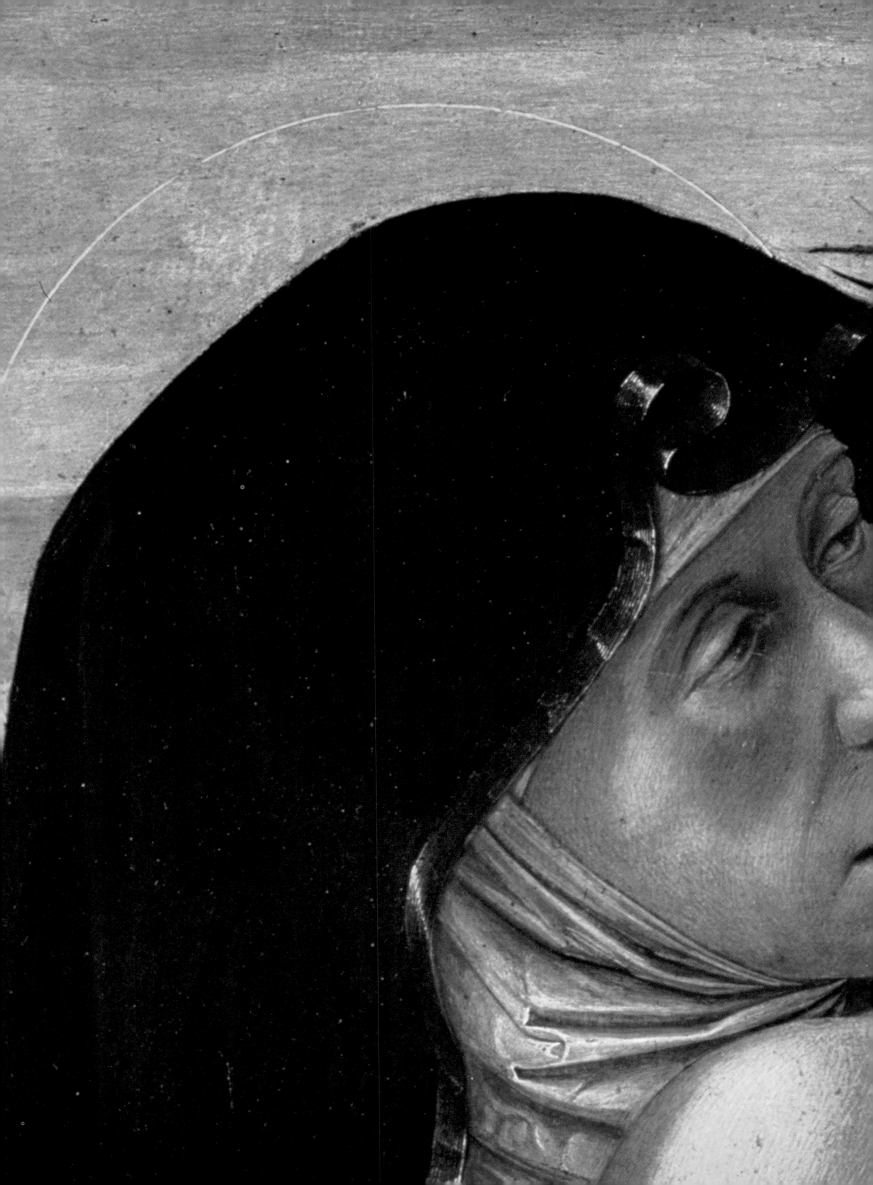

Botticelli's art has been described as delicate, musical, dream-like, and melancholy. He was only a few years younger than Lorenzo the Magnificent, and was perhaps the artist most closely linked with the Medici circle. His two famous allegorical paintings— Primavera and The Birth of Venus— were painted for Lorenzo's cousin, Lorenzo di Pierfrancesco, and were placed in his villa at Castello. Botticelli used an undulating, clear-cut, and exquisite line to explicate the neo-platonic ideal of a spirit which must be released from the material world to achieve divinity. Beauty, here symbolized by Venus, is the principle governing the universe.

Pages 62-63
Sandro Botticelli, The Birth of Venus, 1482-84, panel, Florence, Uffizi

Pages 64-65
Sandro Botticelli, The Birth of Venus, detail of the goddess's face

Pages 66-67
Sandro Botticelli, **Primavera**, *detail with the Three Graces, Cupid, and Flora*

Flora almost seems to have emerged from the poetry of Poliziano, who wrote of her honest figure, her modest dress decorated with roses, flowers, and grass, and the ringlets accenting her forehead.

Pages 68-69
Vittore Carpaccio, The
Arrival of the Ambassadors,
*1490-95, from the series
of large canvases showing*
The Legend of St. Ursula,
Venice, Academy

*The Venetian painter
Carpaccio placed miraculous
stories in an immediate,
understandable reality by
paying careful attention to
detail in clothes, furnishings,
attitudes, and fashions.*

Pages 70-71
Vittore Carpaccio, details from
The Legend of St. Ursula

The Italian term teleri
*(literally, "textiles") is used to
describe large canvases of
linen or hemp mounted on
frames and used for painting
in Venice toward the end of
the fifteenth century. The
greater elasticity of the canvas
made the paintings more
resistant to humidity.*

*Carpaccio (the official painter
in Venice, along with Gentile
Bellini) used this technique
with great success. In this
view of the city, he used bright
colors, foreshortening of
houses and palaces, and a
crowd of personalities, all
executed in minute detail.
The splendid force of Vittore's
color came to mark the
Venetian school of painting.*

Pages 72-73
Domenico Ghirlandaio, The
Legend of St. Fina, *1475,
fresco, San Gimignano,
Collegiata Church*

*For Ghirlandaio, as for
Carpaccio, painting combined
reality with religious teaching.
Here, in this burial scene, the
medieval towers of San
Gimignano appear above the
city skyline.*

Pages 74-75
Domenico Ghirlandaio, The Legend of St. Fina, *detail*

Pages 76-77
Niccolo dell' Arca, Pietà,
1485, terra-cotta, Bologna,
Santa Maria della Vita

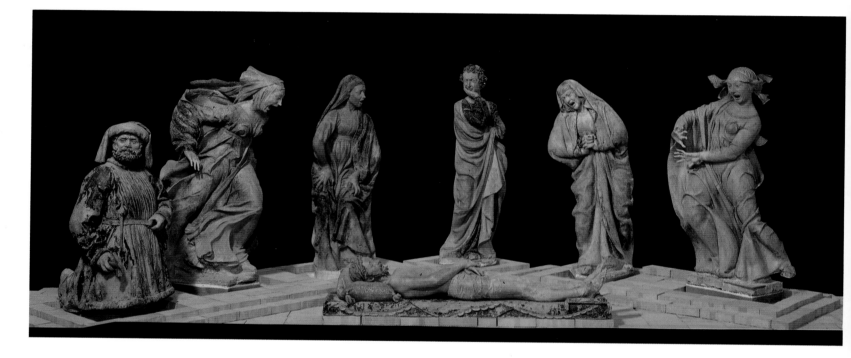

Niccolo dell' Arca's work is
considered to mark sculpture's
transition into the sharp and
dynamic work of the Ferrara
school of painting. He came
from Apulia but worked
mainly in central Italy.
Niccolo produced this Pietà
with strong contrast,
theatricality, and previously
unseen dramatic strength. His
frenzied, grieving Mary
Magdalene acts, through her
disheveled clothing, as a
tribute to the popular
medieval tradition of sacred
representations.

Pages 78-79
Niccolo dell' Arca, Pietà,
detail

Jacopo della Quercia, Tomb of
Ilaria del Caretto, *1406,*
marble, Lucca, Cathedral of
San Martino

Here is an equally exciting
sculpture formed in a
completely different way,
showing tenderness and a
vague melancholy. The figure
of the young Ilaria has come to
symbolize the humanist tomb.

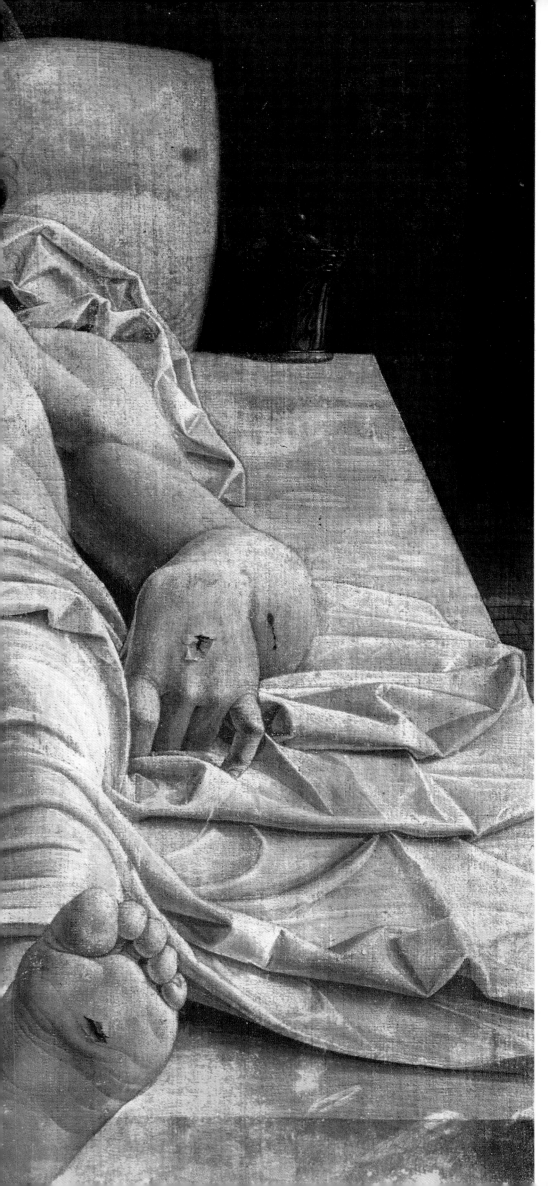

Pages 82-83
Andrea Mantegna, Dead Christ, *late fifteenth century, canvas, Milan, Brera Art Gallery*

Notice the bold, harsh foreshortening of this impressive view of the crucified Jesus. A Venetian artist, Mantegna is universally known for his frescoes in the Gonzaga ducal palace in Mantua. There, too, skilled foreshortening and the imaginative use of perspective illustrate a refined and cultured world, filled by a subtle melancholy. In this religious work, on the other hand, everything is dramatically tense. The viewer can read in it omens of further death and crisis which developed following the death of Savonarola at the stake.

*Pages 84-85
Michelangelo, The Madonna
of the Steps, 1490-95,
marble, Florence, Casa
Buonarotti*

*Giorgio Vasari, the biographer
of Italian artists, called
Michelangelo "divine."
He was not even twenty years
old when he sculpted
The Madonna of the Steps
and The Battle of the
Centaurs. These masterpieces
show clearly that sculpture is
produced not by placing the
material on a surface, as in
painting, but by raising it.
They show Michelangelo's
extraordinary skill, especially
remarkable given both his
youth and the different
techniques used. For the
Madonna, he follows a
technique similar to that used
by Donatello. In The Battle
of the Centaurs
(a mythological theme
suggested to him by
Poliziano), he shows total
confidence in producing an
energetic tangle of moving
and grasping naked bodies,
which can be considered a
prelude to the themes he
developed in his later years.*

Pages 86-87
Michelangelo, The Battle of
the Centaurs, *1490-95,
marble, Florence, Casa
Buonarotti*

A WORSHIP
OF NATURE

This painting, showing the moment before the storm actually arrives, is full of symbolism which has not yet been fully deciphered. Like The Three Philosophers *and* The Concert Champetre, The Tempest *is a small painting designed for the enjoyment of* *the buyer in his private home—a type of painting which was to have great success in the future. The ambiguity of the subjects reveals both the personality of the artist and the wish of the buyer for a work accessible to a small circle of cultured and* *refined friends.*

Vasari said that Giorgione was born to put the spirit into figures and to illustrate the freshness of the living. He presents us with a new pictorial language. The landscape absorbs the horizon and the human figure tends to reflect the smoothness of the natural space. The wavering forms of his work, the warm and soft colors, the melancholy mood which runs through figures and landscapes, are all part of an attempt to create a work that is both accessible to the viewer and peaceful to view.

Pages 90-91
Giorgione, The Tempest, *1505-10, canvas, Venice, Galleria dell' Accademia*

Pages 92-93
Giorgione, The Castelfranco
Madonna, *panel, 1504-10,*
Cathedral, Castelfranco
Veneto; details with St.
Liberale and the Madonna

Compared with the traditional arrangement of the Madonna enthroned among the saints, Giorgione represents her against a natural background, which immediately attracts the eye because of its contrast with the Madonna's green dress and red cloak.

The composition is reduced to a simple triangular scheme and the saints—here limited to two—seem lost in their own thoughts.

MOVING BEYOND
MATERIAL LIMITATIONS

Pages 94-95
Michelangelo, Moses, 1515-
16, marble, Rome, San Pietro
in Vincoli

*This statue is part of the
complex marble group designed
by Michelangelo for the tomb
of Pope Julius II. This
construction virtually obsessed
the artist for more than thirty
years. At the start of the
sixteenth century, the Pope had
entrusted to Michelangelo the
task of building his mausoleum.
It was to have been placed in
St. Peter's for the eternal glory
both of the Pope and of the
church itself. Michelangelo was
forced to interrupt the project
several times—for instance,
when he was given the
commission to decorate the
Sistine Chapel. In later years he
suggested a new version of the
mausoleum, but because he was
out of favor with the Pope's
heirs, the project was not
completed until the 1540s; the
scale was much smaller than
originally planned and it was
placed in the Church of San
Pietro in Vincoli rather than in
St. Peter's.*

*The superb statue of Moses,
dated 1515-16, is at the center
of the final version of the tomb.
It is the sculptural corollary of
the powerful illustrations of the
prophets in the Sistine Chapel.
These figures symbolize the
super-human force that is
necessary to liberate mankind
from the material world to
reach the spiritual world.*

THE DIVINE MICHELANGELO

*Pages 96-97
Michelangelo, Pietà, 1497-
1500, marble, Vatican City,
St. Peter's*

*This well-known **Pietà** is
found in St. Peter's and was
sculpted at the end of the
fifteenth century. The tender,
sad face of the young mother
as she holds her dead son in
her arms—just as she held
him when he was a child—
gives to this work a poignancy
that is greater than in
anything else by this artist.
All the artist's attention here
was focused on evoking the
ideal of spiritual beauty which
was so important in the time
of the Florentine Medicis,
a period of which
Michelangelo is one of the
most representative artists.*

THE PRIVATE ROOMS OF JULIUS II

*Pages 98-99
Raphael,* Debate on the Blessed Sacrament, *1509, fresco, Vatican City, Stanza della Segnatura*

Raphael began decorating the apartments of Pope Julius II with the Stanza della Segnatura, the study and private library where he signed and sealed official documents. The themes were chosen by the Pope and were worked out with the help of a neo-platonic philosopher. The intention was to glorify Truth, Beauty, and Goodness through allegories of theology, philosophy, justice, and poetry, using illustrations of historical characters who had distinguished themselves in various fields. Raphael gave many of these figures the features of the great men of his

time; Pope Gregory IX has Pope Julius II's face, da Vinci's face appears on the figure of Plato, and so on. In the second room, the Heliodorus, the frescoes show a series of heavenly interventions on behalf of the church.

Pages 100-101
Raphael, The Liberation of
St. Peter, *detail, 1514, fresco,
Rome, Vatican City, Stanza
dell' Eliodoro*

Pages 102-103
Raphael, Parnassus, *1510-11,*
fresco, Rome, Vatican City,
Stanze

TITIAN'S WOMEN

This work did not receive its best-known title until the seventeenth century. It has been interpreted in various ways, including a reading of it as an allegory of pagan and Christian beauty. It shows the strong expressiveness of Titian, who was twenty-five years old when he painted it. He clearly wanted to work with the contrast between horizontal and vertical lines, the reserved beauty of the clothed woman and the opulent beauty of the nude, and the presence of the sarcophagus as a symbol of death against the fountain, an equally strong symbol of life.

Pages 106-107
Titian, Danae, 1545-46, oil on canvas, Naples, Capodimonte Museum

Titian had many powerful clients, including doges and kings, cardinals and pontiffs. Among the most important was Pope Paul III's nephew, Cardinal Alexander Farnese, for whom the painter took up the theme of the Danae. Along with Venus, the Danae were among the mythological subjects he most loved. The skillful use of color, combined with the strongly sensual quality of the large nude, makes this a work of tremendous charm.

MEDITATIONS ON DEATH

Pages 108-109
Michelangelo, tomb of
Lorenzo de' Medici, Duke of
Urbino, 1524-34, Florence, St.
Lorenzo's Church, new
sacristy, with statues of Dawn
and Evening at Lorenzo's feet

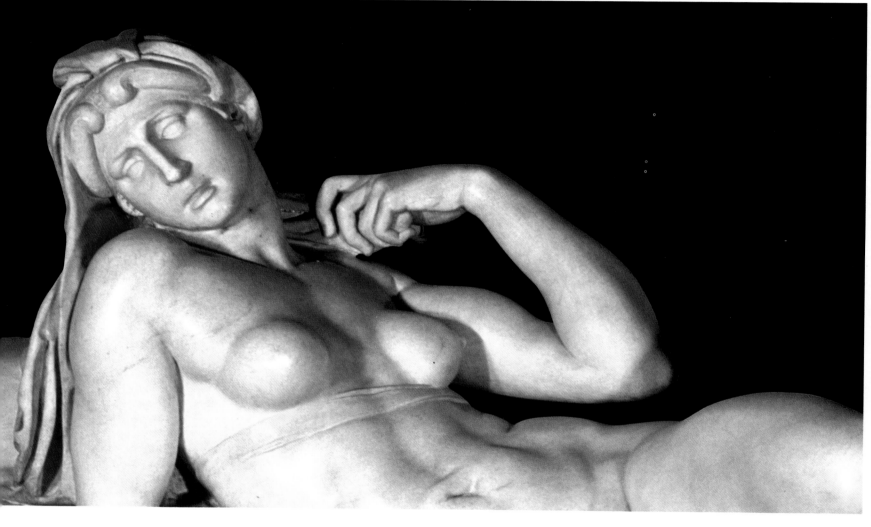

Pages 110-111
Lorenzo Lotto, Portrait of a
Gentleman, *c. 1527, canvas,*
Venice, Gallerie dell'
Accademia

This painting is filled with
information about the
gentleman in the portrait for
those who can read it.
The masterpiece shows signs
of great refinement in the
ribbons, compasses, a ring,
letters, a lady's soft shawl, and
the petals of a withered rose.
Scholar Anna Banti has
written that the gentleman
illustrated must have had an
extremely secretive character!

Pages 112-113
Raphael, Portrait of Julius II, 1511-12, panel, Florence, Uffizi

At the same time that he was decorating the Vatican Stanze, Raphael was also busy with a series of portraits, which he saw as simple displays of affection for friends and acquaintances or dutiful gestures toward patrons. Among these works is the famous portrait of Julius II della Rovere, who is shown as a solitary old man still full of energy and dignity. This portrait, of the Pope reveals the way in which the Urbino-born artist saw the human figure. Raphael's figures, unlike Michelangelo's, were not torn between the physical and the spiritual worlds; rather, he saw them as having achieved interior balance. In this portrait, attention was also given to the psychological state of the subject. His obvious energy, wealth, and strength of character displays Julius II's self-confidence despite his great age; his surroundings, from his clothing to his numerous rings, support this impression.

GUIDO RENI: TRANSPARENCY AND SENSUALITY

Pages 116-117
Guido Reni, Atalante and Ippomene, *canvas, Naples, Capodimonte Museum*

A Bolognese artist who combined the opposing schools of the Caracci brothers and Caravaggio, Guido Reni seems to look back to the Mannerists in this mythological painting.
His transparent overlays, the use of cold colors and unusual shades, the crossing lines, and the diagonally traced bodies reveal a uniquely subtle, somewhat nervous style of painting.

TWO DESCENTS FROM THE CROSS

Page 118 and following
Jacopo Carucci, known as Pontormo, Descent from the Cross, *c. 1526, panel, Florence, Santa Felicità*

Softness and angularity, sinuous lines and broken outlines, cold colors set against warm and contrasting colors: these elements provide two contrasting perspectives on the Sacred Story. These parallel and entirely contemporary works of art by Pontormo and Rosso Fiorentino are by two artists considered perfect representatives of the purest form of Tuscan Mannerism.

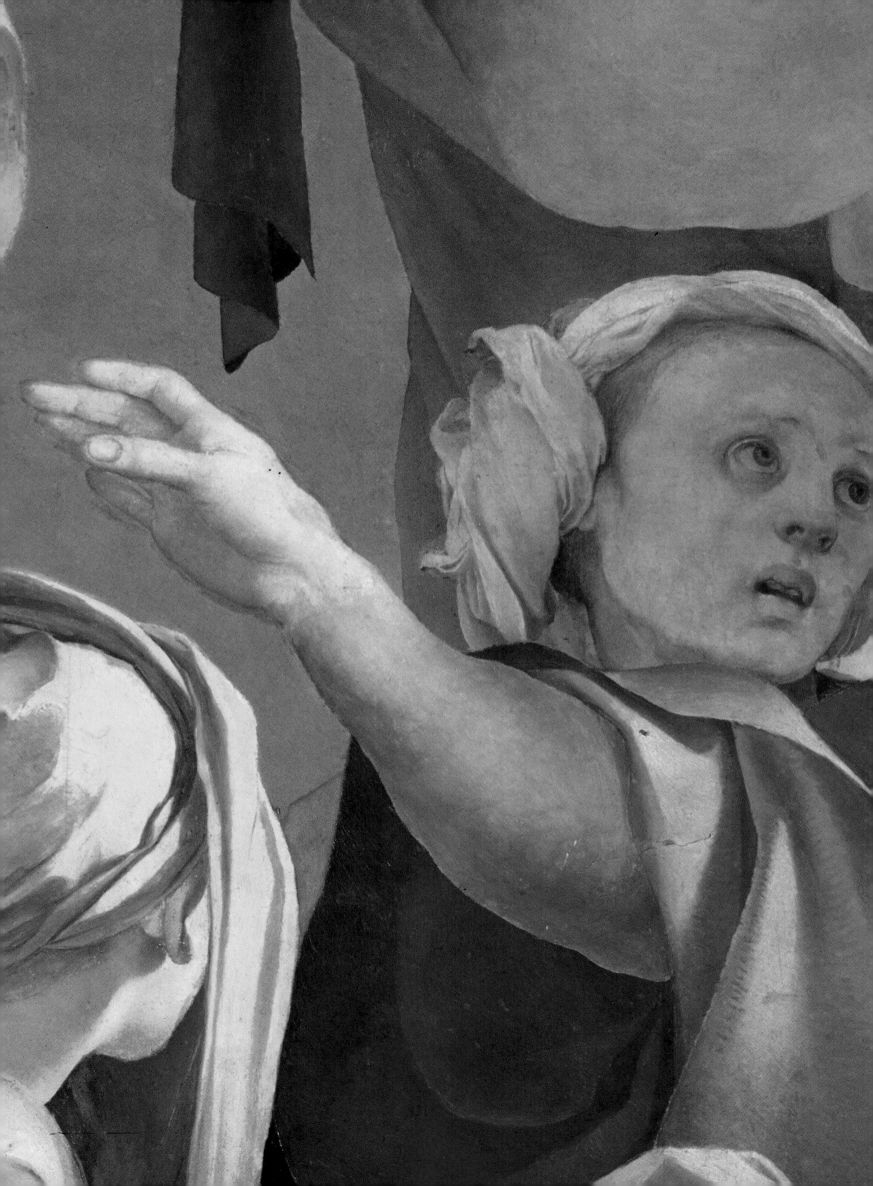

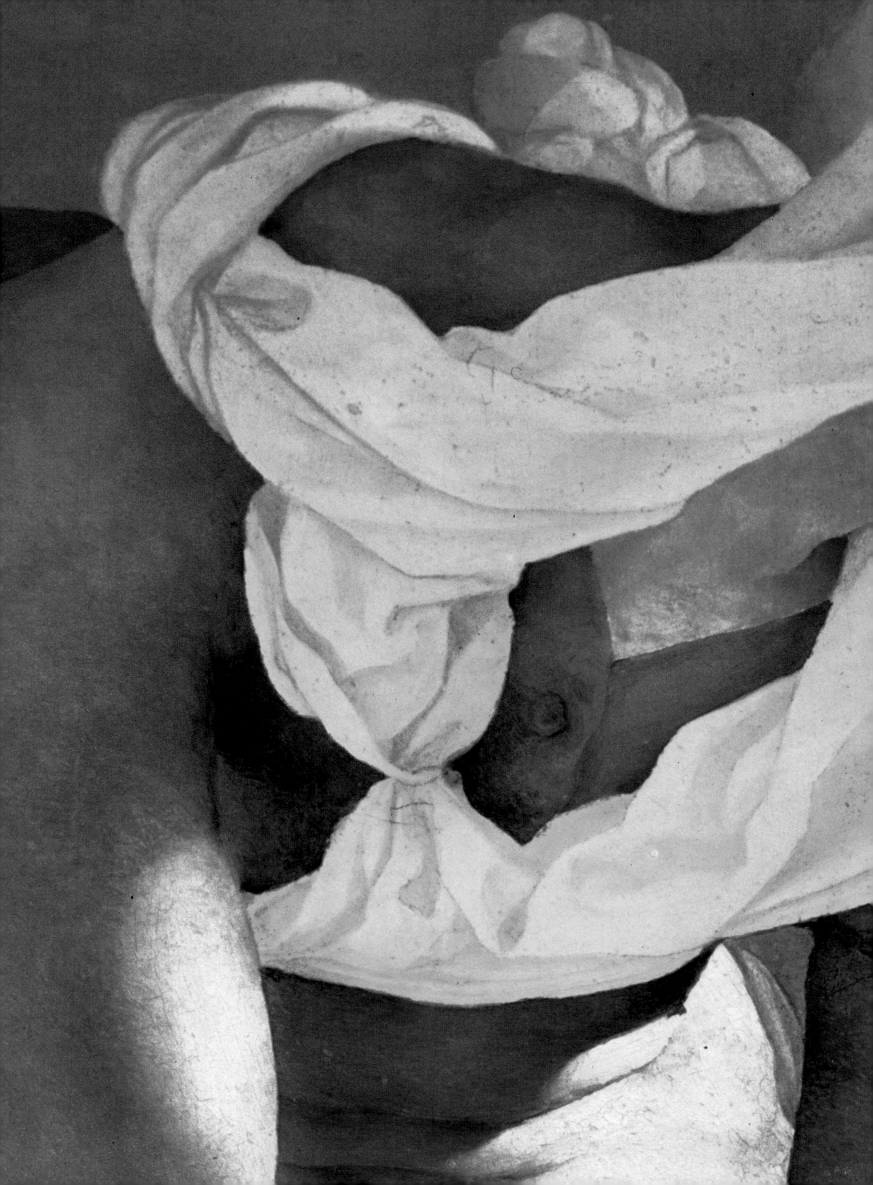

Page 124 and following
Rosso Fiorentino, **Descent**
from the Cross, *1521, pane*
Volterra, Pinacoteca

AMONG LEAVES
AND FLOWERS

Pages 128-129
Antonio Allegri, known as
Coreggio, decoration of the
Abbess's room, 1519, fresco,
Parma, Convent of St. Paul

Allegri's first commission,
from the cultivated Abbess
Giovanna Piacenza, was
obtained before he reached the
age of thirty. This painter of
style and grace decorated a
room in her convent.
Originality, pictorial
freshness, and illusionism
serve to create a flowering
pergola, encircled by putti and
cupids in a whirl of colors.
More than a place of spiritual
retreat, the convent of St. Paul
also served as an elegant
meeting place for the ladies of
Parma's high society. The
figurative playfulness of the
vault (which becomes a
pergola dense with vegetation
with openings that enclose
sculptures similar to real
figures) shows the contrast
between truth and fiction,
nature and art—art that is a
joy for the eyes and an
ornament for a noble and
exquisite society.

Pages 130-131
Coreggio, the Abbess's room,
detail of the vault

Page 132
Jacopo Robusti, known as
Tintoretto, Saint Mark
Rescuing the Saracen, *1563-*
66, for the Scuola di San
Marco, oil on canvas, Venice,
Gallerie dell' Accademia

Page 133
Tintoretto, Removal of the
Body of St. Mark, *1563-66,*
for the Scuola di San Marco,
oil on canvas, Venice, Gallerie
dell' Accademia

The son of a cloth dyer from whom he took the nickname Tintoretto ("the tinted one"), Jacopo Robusti accepted the teachings of the Mannerist school. He studied the works of Michelangelo and, above all, was fascinated by the theatrical element which became the dominant keynote of his work. With his large canvases for the Scuola Grande di San Marco he became an important part of the Venetian scene. He received praise from discerning critic Pietro Aretino because of his entirely original use of theatricality and spectacular scenes. In the paintings depicting scenes from the life of St. Mark, Tintoretto pursued the theme of supernatural intervention as both a wonder and a miracle, a theme which became dominant in his work. His very dynamic scenes feature strong contrasts of light and oblique flights into the distance, both surprising and emotionally involving the spectator. In this amazing new way of representing the miraculous, Tintoretto heralded some of the favorite themes of the Baroque period.

In 1573, Veronese painted a Last Supper for the convent of San Zanipolo. It met with the disapproval of the Inquisition because of the unconventional images the artist had introduced into the religious picture, and because he was suspected of practicing Lutheran heresy. When asked whether he thought it fitting that the painting should include "buffoons, drunkards, German soldiers, dwarfs, and other similar scurrilities," Veronese answered that painters were permitted the same license as poets and madmen; then he saved his painting by changing its title to The Feast in the House of Levi. Anticipating much modern theory on the use of color, Veronese discovered the luminous effect created by juxtaposing complementary shades such as ruby red with emerald green, and yellow with violet, to created a gratifyingly pleasing effect. The greatest example of this method is seen, perhaps, in the frescoes in the Villa Barbaro-Volpi at Maser near Treviso.

Pages 138-139
Paolo Veronese, The Feast in
the House of Levi, *detail*

Page 140
Michelangelo Merisi da
Caravaggio, The Calling of
Saint Matthew, *1599-1600,*
canvas, Rome, San Luigi dei
Francesi, Cappella contarelli

Page 141
Caravaggio, St. Matthew
and the Angel, *1602, canvas,*
Rome, San Luigi dei
Francesci, Capella Contarelli

In this work, the story of Saint
Matthew's martyrdom is set
in the time of the artist; the
people in the picture are
dressed in clothes of the
1600s. Like Masaccio,
Caravaggio used contem-
porary settings in this way
to enhance the Christian
experience. The light has a
new and strong value, an
expressiveness never before
seen. Similarly, the
composition with St. Matthew
and the angel shows
originality in the way in
which the saint is surprised at
his work as the angel dictates
to him the genealogy of
Christ.

Pages 142-143
Caravaggio, Rest During the Flight into Egypt, c. 1593, canvas, Dome, Galleria Doria Pamphili

Caravaggio is noted for the tremendous power of his painting and his novel way of avoiding every convention and academic tradition. Nevertheless, he offers a landscape with muted colors, glimpses of nature in the foreground, and an atmosphere of domestic intimacy and tenderness as the Virgin and Child are put to sleep by music played by the angel.

Pages 144-145
Caravaggio, Basket of Fruit, c. 1596, canvas, Milan, Pinacoteca Ambrosiana

Pages 146-147
Gianlorenzo Bernini, Apollo
and Daphne, 1622-25,
marble, Rome, Galleria
Borghese

Pages 148-149
Gianlorenzo Bernini, David,
detail, 1623, marble, Rome,
Galleria Borghese

Tremendous energy and a
strong view of the world made
it possible for this great
Neapolitan sculptor and
architect, mainly active at
the papal court, to bring
a new vision to sculpture.
With a series of monumental
groups commissioned by
Cardinal Scipione Borghese

(one of the most brilliant
patrons of the arts of the time)
for his villa-museum, this
artist was able to show his
skill. Among his works for
Borghese are the twisted
statue of David and the group
of Apollo and Daphne, which
takes the verses of Ovid's
Metamorphoses and shapes
it into marble. Through
Bernini's ability, the marble
came to seem almost as
transparent as alabaster.

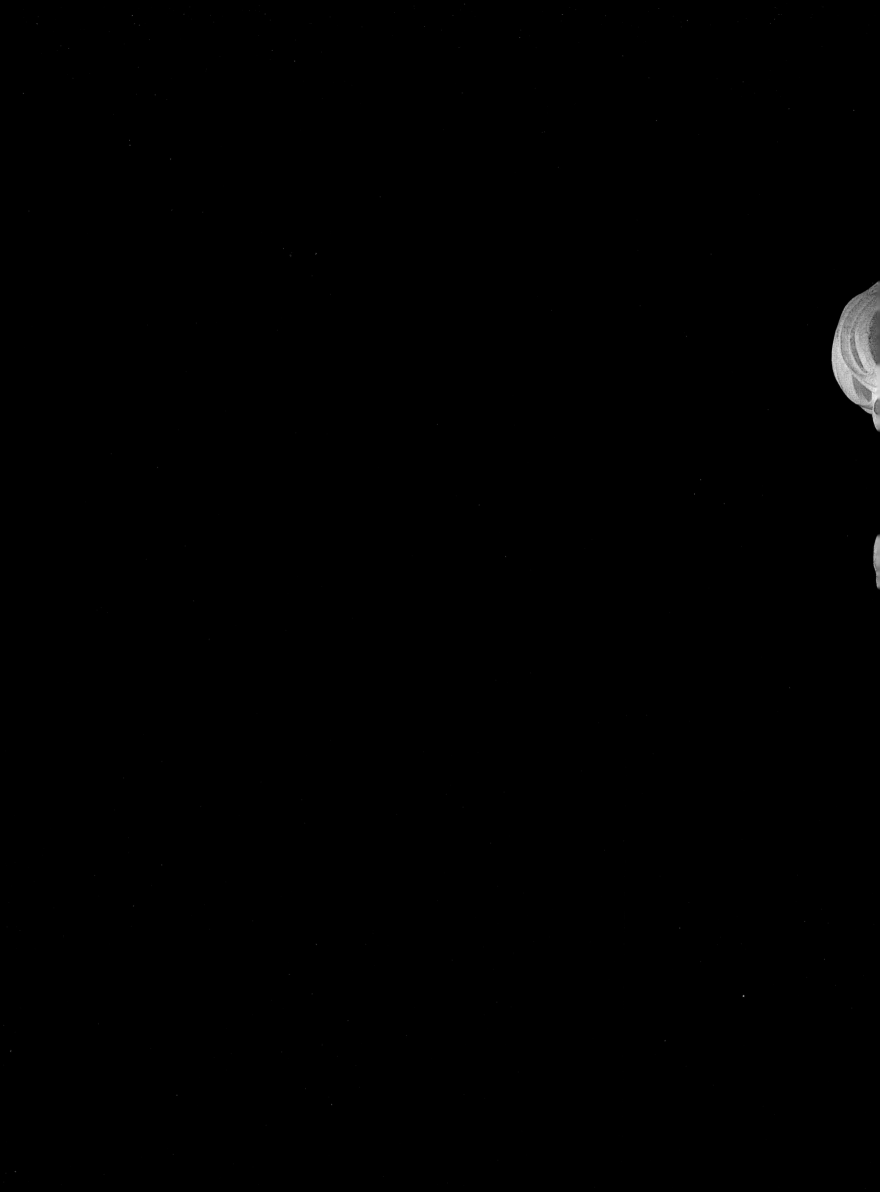

Pages 150-151
Antonio Canova, Paolina
Borghese Bonaparte as
Victorious Venus,
*1804-1808, marble, Rome,
Galleria Borghese*

*The Neoclassical ideal of
sublime beauty, for which the
artist constantly strives, can
be seen in this famous
sculpture of the wife of Prince
Camillo Borghese and sister
of Napoleon. Canova put a
thin layer of wax over the
nude statue to give the marble
a pinkish transparency.
In addition to this evocation*

*of the softness of flesh
(the same which we find in
his famous* Three Graces*),
Canova created a slight
feeling that the features of the
face are actually quivering.
The half-closed lips and the
softness of the cushions
combine to evoke a subtle
eroticism.*

Pages 152-153
Antonio Canova, Paolina
Borghese Bonaparte as
Victorious Venus, *detail*

151

The Appeal of

the Sacred

THE APPEAL OF THE SACRED

There is nothing that equals the continuous historical importance of the Church, which from the beginning of the Christian era brought both culture and art to Italian life. Today it may be difficult to imagine what churches once meant for the people. The building itself was often the only stone building within a wide area, the only building of any importance. Its towers served as a reference point for people traveling from a distance. During religious ceremonies, the citizens of a city would gather in the church; the contrast between the tall building, replete with paintings and sculptures, and the humble homes where they spent their everyday lives must have been overwhelmingly dramatic. One can understand why communities took so much interest in the construction of their churches and why they took so much pride in the richness of their decoration.

The building of a church often took place over a period of years or even decades, and in economic terms transformed an entire city. The quarrying of the stone and its transport, the preparation of scaffolding, the employment of wandering craftsmen who brought not only their skills but also stories of distant lands. . . . all represented an event of real economic importance.

The construction of the first basilicas created the need for a large symbolic repertory from which artists could draw in order that the holy word could be spread to everyone. The Old Testament, with its scope and wealth of events, was from the beginning the source of a great deal of inspiration for Christian artists. It is also believed that the earliest Christian symbols — the dove, fish, and lyre — were borrowed from pagan iconography, with symbolic meanings which often proved difficult to interpret.

Pages 154-155
Venice, St. Mark's Basilica,
eleventh century, detail of the
spire, statues on the façade

Pages 156-157
Rome, St. Cosmas and St.
Damian, sixth century,
mosaic in the apse

157

Page 158
*Sacra di San Michele, Susa,
twelfth century, detail of the
sculpted decoration of a
window*

The Sacra di San Michele, one
of the most singular
Romanesque buildings in the
region, is located at the
entrance to the Susa valley. In
the Middle Ages, this valley
was a busy route for pilgrims
and for crusaders heading for
ports before sailing to the
Holy Land. Lombardian,
Ligurian and Tuscan
merchants also used this
route. According to tradition,
the Benedictine Abbey was
founded in 988 A.D. It was in
a strategic position of great
importance, and became not
only a destination for pilgrims
but also the central defense of
the population, as indicated by
the walls around it. The
church itself gives the effect of
a fortress and is built on a
very high base which also
contains the monastery
buildings. The sculptural
decoration is of great interest.
There is a monumental
staircase and a portal sculpted
in the first half of the twefth
century with doorposts
bearing the symbols of the
constellations and the signs of
the zodiac.

Pope Gregory the Great, living in the middle of the sixth century A.D., believed that painting could be as great in value to the illiterate as writing was to those who could read. Since many members of the church could neither read nor write, the paintings served the same purpose as an illustrated book can serve a child. The subjects were presented in as clear and simple a way as possible, excluding everything which might distract from their basic religious purpose.

For much of the Middle Ages, Christian iconography consisted of decorated manuscripts and liturgical texts and illustrated books. The creativity of the artist was therefore somewhat limited, until Giotto at Padua and Duccio da Buoninsegna at Siena, viewing the conventional figurative themes from another angle, advanced religious art with their detailed, realistic, paintings.

During the Renaissance, and even more clearly during the Baroque era, the artist became progressively more detached from the subject, and artistic works became more independent of traditional religious iconography. While the formal links are maintained, the content of the work often varies from traditional schemes. In some cases, there is a partial or total extraction of the theological content; this changed the relationship between culture and religion, which until that point had more or less coincided. While the subject of art remained religious, it reflected the problems of the artist and embraced the philosophical, scientific, and cultural elements of the age in which he lived.

Stylistic Developments

After the edict of Constantine in 313 A.D. that decreed the full liberalization of the Christian religion, a standard typology for churches was established. These first churches were basilicas with a longitudinal plan. Various theories have been put forward to explain the choice of such a design, but the most valid, perhaps, is that which suggests that architectural elements from the pagan world were adjusted to meet the needs of the new religion. At the same time, there came in from the Near East churches which had a central plan, originally used for small buildings and later for churches of quite remarkable size. During the Medieval period, the basilica plan was dominant in both Romanesque and Gothic churches, although often in different versions.

Churches with a central plan became increasingly important during the Renaissance. The cultural environment which favored this plan also fostered the emergence of philosophical ideas, studies, and treatises about man and his central role in the order and rationality of nature. Furthermore, a renewed interest in the studies of classicism and a careful study of the works of Vitruvio supported the view that man, enclosed in a circle or square, was the symbol of the universe.

During the seventeenth century, religious building design was subjected to the influence of two different but connected movements. The Counter Reformation movement supported the need for preaching and propagandizing in the renewed church; the other movement reflected a different artistic feeling and an altered spiritual sensibility, and aimed at expressing the church triumphant. This led to an increase in the number of churches which consisted of only a single large area without chapels and excessive decoration; on the other hand, there was a marked preference for centralized or *elliptical plans that represented an attempt to open the religion to the people. Bernini's vision of space, for instance, reflects this feeling.*

Romanesque and Gothic Cathedrals

After the year 1000 A.D., when the irrational fear of the millennium had passed, Europe saw an exceptional building fervor. This was tied to an increase in population, economic development, and the investment of treasures accumulated over the centuries or brought back from expeditions to the Orient. Cathedrals have been called the first great financial effort of the new Europe. A German monk, Rudolf, addressed this phenomenon. He pointed out that all over the world, and especially in Italy and France, people were rebuilding churches not because it was necessary but rather in a competition to see who had the best buildings. In France alone, eighty cathedrals and five hundred large churches were built over the course of three centuries. Those who took part in the building received religious indulgences.

The enthusiasm for this movement was compared by the twentieth-century architect Le Courbusier to the enthusiasm of the modern world as advances in technology brought countries closer together. Europe, he felt, had at the millennium organized crafts into a search for new techniques which led to both unexpected and unknown forms. A universal language favored the exchange of culture from the West to the East and from the North to the South. In a similar way the twentieth century was able to bring diverse cultures together.

In Romanesque and Norman churches, round arches usually rest on solid pillars. The general impression that these churches give both internally and externally is that of massive power. They have little decoration, few windows, strong walls, and towers reminiscent of medieval fortresses. These huge masses of stone, built by the church in a land of farmers and warriors who had only recently converted from paganism, seemed to express the concept of a militant church. These buildings offered shelter from the assaults of evil; according to this concept, the duty of the church on earth was to fight the powers of darkness until the Day of Judgement, when the hour of triumph for the church would come. The structural revolution of the Romanesque style was based on a technique which must have appeared extremely daring. In Sant' Ambrogio in Milan and in many cathedrals in the Lombardy area, the roof has a system of cross vaults. It is no longer separate from the walls, but joins with them to constitute a unique mass and image.

The cathedrals, built as they were over decades, were active building sites watched enthusiastically by the citizenry. In these hives of activity, architects acted at one and the same time as contractors, urban planners, and engineers. Some of them became heroes in their own days, such as Lanfranco, builder of Mantova Cathedral. He was described as both mirabilis artifex *and* magnificus aedificator — *an admirable artist and a magnificent builder.*

The basic building materials, chosen from those available in the region, were normally left with their natural surfaces. Only the sculptures would sometimes receive a delicate polychromatic protective covering. The masons, organized into corporations based on secret codes and various degrees of initiation from the apprentices up to the master, met in lodges at the base of

the cathedral. This base was a covered workshop where they could continue working during the winter. The building under construction was directly controlled by the Chapter, a group of canons who were independent of the bishop. Normally, the cathedral was not only the guiding center of religious life, but also the center of civic life (along with the town hall and the market square). In the aisles of these religious buildings one could have discussions and do business; during this period, the church drew nearer than it had ever been before to being the multi-functional equivalent of the pagan basilicas.

As well as being the symbol of the bishop and the religion, the cathedral was also the pride of the entire town and came to express strength as well as faith. There were even some fortified churches which, in times of need, could give shelter to the inhabitants of the town. It has been said that every cathedral should be viewed as a safe refuge, representing the military vocation of a feudal society. One commentator said that the Gothic cathedral is bourgeois and urban, while the Romanesque is monastic and aristocratic. The bourgeois aspect of the Gothic cathedral arose because the lay community came to play more and more of a part in the building of cathedrals, which in themselves could never have existed without the wealth of the cities.

From the thirteenth century on, Gothic architecture introduced new techniques which represented more than just technical developments. The pillars alone became sufficient to hold up the ribs of the vault; the stones between only filled the space, making it unnecessary to build massively thick walls. It was possible to build a framework in stone that could hold the entire construction. All that was needed were slender pillars and narrow vaulting ribs — there was no longer any need for heavy stone walls and, indeed, wide windows could be added. Soon, structures in stone and glass could be constructed, unlike anything previously known. This was the inspiration for the Gothic cathedral. Using flying buttresses to complete the ribbing of the vault, the Gothic cathedral was able to appear suspended within its stone structure.

Standing inside a Gothic cathedral, we can see the complex play of compression and tension which sustains the high vault; there are no walls or massive pillars blocking our view. These new cathedrals gave the faithful a vision that almost matched Revelations, with its prophesy of pearl doors, priceless gems, and roads of pure gold and transparent glass. In the Gothic period, it seemed as if this vision had come down from heaven to earth. The walls of these buildings were not cold and unpleasant but rich with beautiful windows which shone like precious stones. The believer who abandoned himself to this beauty could feel close to understanding the mysteries of the Kingdom of Heaven. Even from a distance, these buildings seemed to proclaim the Heavenly Host and the prestige of a triumphant church.

The Central Plan Renaissance Church

The history of science is of basic importance to the story of humanism. When Filippo Brunelleschi became the director of building for the Cathedral of Santa Maria del Fiore in Florence, he was supposed to use the original foundation created by the Gothic architects: an octagonal cupola with equilateral ribs along with the mystical significance of that Marian crown. However, he used a radically new and different method. He was unable to use traditional scaffolding that rested on the ground, nor were specialized craftsmen available. This led to a variety of amazing inventions. The dome was built with suspended scaffolding, and the building site was organized in an almost industrial way.

Aside from Brunelleschi's technological inventions, the political value of the building also upset medieval perspectives. The dome, Leon Battista Alberti said, seemed to cover all the people of Tuscany with its shadow, reflecting the new imperialistic will of Florence. In this aspect, the cathedral revealed itself as "state architecture" beyond feudalism, aiming for both national and regional hegemony.

Despite its being added onto the base of the Gothic cathedral, the dome of Santa Maria del Fiore is the first great temple built upon the central plan as developed by humanism, first in architectural theory and later in actual practice. It was Leon Battista Alberti especially who, in the mid-fifteenth century, codified a new vision of space which changed not only the spatial but also the religious view of the Gothic cathedral.

The Great Hall Churches of the Counter Reformation

The history of Saint Peter's in Rome reflects the contrast between the styles of churches. The first plans, developed by Giuliano da Sangallo and Fra' Giocondo were, respectively, a cross inside a square and a basilica similar to St. Mark's in Venice. After the actual building had begun a debate started; over the course of the sixteenth century it became a real argument. Numerous plans were presented by many architects, including Raphael, which had the aim of transforming Bra-

Pages 164-165
Pavia, Chartreuse, Giovanni
Solari, fifteenth century

Page 166
Filippo Brunelleschi, Capella
dei Pazzi in Santa Croce,
Florence, fifteenth century,
interior

mante's temple into a basilica. The nave was finally built by Carlo Maderno. It should be remembered in any discussion of the building of St. Peter's that it was the selling of indulgences for this colossal building which provoked Martin Luther's protest and Rome's reply, changing the course of Christianity.

Following the radical movement led by the German monk against the absurd and almost Babylonian splendor of the Roman church and after the Reformation and the sack of Rome in 1527, the Vatican took a series of countermeasures. These involved the foundation of other new religious orders, a reorganization of other orders through the Society of Jesus (the Jesuits, founded 1534), the revival of the Inquisition, and the setting up of the Holy Office. It was, however, primarily the Council of Trent (1545-1563) which established the strategies for regaining lost credibility through a new way of viewing religion.

At the same time, the church exercised a rigid control over art. Primarily because of the strong Jesuit influence, a new type of hall began to be built. This type of church was considered the most suitable for preaching, and the Council of Trent considered it a way of attracting the masses to the church. The Chiesa del Gesù in Rome (1568-1573) can be considered both the prototype and the conclusion to a debate that had lasted centuries.

The result was reached in the end by the contrasts between the needs of the Jesuits and Cardinal Alessandro Farnese, its powerful commissioner and financier. The Society of Jesus was able to impose the already tried and tested design of the church; the Cardinal, in his turn, was able to ensure that the hall was vaulted like the transept of St. Peter's rather than having the flat roof suggested by the Jesuits. Once this compromise had been reached it was left to the selected architect, Vignola, to give formal definition to a type of church which was to find great favor throughout the entire Catholic world. The history of the Chiesa del Gesù had a significant influence on later architecture; various treatises printed from the middle of the sixteenth century onward praised the design of the church and its construction. Cardinal Borromeo, for instance, urged bishops to consult with an architect in designing churches, and also urged that the building should be in the shape of a cross as in the Roman basilicas. Andrea Palladio pointed out the value of the cross shape as well, saying that it represented the cross on which Jesus was crucified.

The Theatrical in the Baroque Church

In the first quarter of the seventeenth century, Saint Peter's became the backdrop to the Roman church's proclamation of triumph after the struggle of the Reformation. In the transept of the Vatican basilica, sumptuous scenes were created to celebrate the heroes of this war. In 1610 a provisional section was built onto the basilica for the canonization of Carlo Borromeo, and in 1622 Ignatius of Loyola, Teresa of Avila, Filippo Neri, and Francesco Saverio were all proclaimed saints at the same time. In 1623 in Saint Peter's, Gianlorenzo Bernini began work on the baldacchino, or canopy, one of the outstanding features of Baroque architecture. Over the course of several decades he redesigned the basilica with sculptures and many colored statues, culminating in the Cathedra itself. Finally, Bernini built the colonnade, which

*Page 169
Francesco Borromini,
Sant'Ivo alla Sapienza, mid-
fourteenth century, Rome,
interior of the dome*

brought a new urban feeling of space to St. Peter's. The colonnade in St. Peter's Square is not only an entrance to the church but also takes the church further into the city. The two rows of columns represent the church embracing the faithful. Bernini felt that the entrance must show that the church welcomes Catholics with open arms as a mother welcomes a child, while it also welcomes heretics and infidels in order to bring them to the truth faith.

Each of Bernini's works can be viewed as part of a great spectacle. Many of his religious sculptures can be viewed as tragic recitations; his architectural efforts have a theatrical element as well. Consider the "theater within the theater" aspect of the Raimondi Chapel in San Pietro in Montorio and the Cornaro Chapel in Santa Maria della Vittoria, where each chapel is a smaller dramatic stage within the larger stage of the church itself. Sant' Andrea al Quirinale provides a total scene and the Church of the Assumption a backdrop to the story of Christianity.

Every means possible was used to spread the religion. The use of light in architecture was important in this respect. During the Middle Ages and into the age of humanism, light was used in a metaphysical way; then it changed into a physical use of light inside a definite space. For Caravaggio, light was an instrument of meditation and, indeed, redemption. In Baroque architecture light was used with such skill that while true light was reflected from bronze and stucco there was also the impression of additional light coming from within the materials themselves.

From time to time, light was made to take on different characteristics: light being reflected; light coming from above, the side, or the back; half-light or dim light; chambers of light — all part of a plan to create theaters of light and sound. When one enters these churches it is possible to understand how the splendor and ostentation of precious stones, gold, and stucco were designed to evoke heavenly glory in a more literal sense than that of medieval cathedrals. The more the Protestants preached against the ostentation of the church, the more anxiously did the church try to acquire the work of the finest artists. Thus the Reformation and its challenge to the cult of images had a direct effect on the development of the Baroque style.

The Roman Catholic church had realized that art could serve religion more broadly than it had in the Middle Ages, when it was limited to teaching the gospel to the illiterate. It was now viewed as a way to convert those who, perhaps, had actually read too much. Architects, sculptors, and painters were called upon to transform the churches into huge art shows of overpowering splendor. These spaces were perfect frames for the sumptuous rites of the Roman Catholic church.

With the fall of Renaissance philosophy, its morality also collapsed. The once seemingly rational hierarchical structure of the universe became relational, and was replaced by more direct and emotional relationships. A new age was born; the relationship between spectator and work of art was completely changed.

With this, Leon Battista Alberti's view of a rigid law-ordered world, in which everything is clearly defined, was no longer adequate. Everything seemed to be rely upon chance; even the categories of aesthetic pleasure changed.

The contemplation of a fifteenth-century masterpiece is based on a static but delicate balance of emo-

Pages 170-171
Rome, Santa Maria Maggiore,
fourth and fifth centuries,
façade

tion and logic. Man, moving from the initial vision, gradually entered into an increasingly subtle world of interpretation, participating psychologically in an interior both secret and harmonious.

In the seventeenth century, man and art lost this balance. In the new forms of architecture, every turn brought a surprise; decoration was based on a variety of perspectives; canvases were loaded with mystery; surfaces formerly a simple white or gray plaster were luxuriously gilded. All these changes were part of a collective turning away from the past. In the seventeenth century, the need for law was felt strongly — but since it could no longer be based on reason it had to be based on consent and on tradition. By insisting on this concept, society was saved from chaos. The art and architecture of the period embody this effort. Beneath the sensuality and rhetoric of religious painting and the splendor of these gilded churches lies the terror of eternal damnation, the need to reinforce the culture, and the desire to create an aura of permanence within the civilization of the period.

Propaganda has never been so much at one with art. At no time since the seventeenth century has the relativity of affirmed values been felt so acutely; nor has the reaction to the dangers of a crisis — the Reformation — been so decisive.

Pages 172-173
Ravenna, San Vitale, sixth century, mosaic decoration of the vault, Emperor Justinian, Bishop Maximiano, and the court

The extreme simplicity of the external architecture contrasts with the richness of the internal decoration. It also contrasts with the complexity of the plan, which is an octagon around a smaller octagon, all opening into an exedra. The principal elements of decoration are the elegant capitals, the marbles, and the mosaics.

Pages 174-175
Ravenna, San Vitale,
The Empress Theodora and
Her Retinue

Pages 176-177
Ravenna, Mausoleum of Galla
Placidia, fifth century,
interior, mosaic over the
entrance showing Christ as
the Good Shepherd

THE CHARM OF THE
BYZANTINE EAST

The fundamental architectural nucleus of the basilica, which we can no longer see, was a large building in the form of a Greek cross topped by five domes. This is the third construction of the basilica, made in the twelfth century as a visible expression of Venetian power.

Pages 178-179
Venice, St. Mark's, eleventh century and later

The decoration uses numerous materials — stone, marble, and bronze — for sculptures, bas-reliefs, and mosaics, and was finished only in the sixteenth century. It somewhat cancels the effect of the thickness of the masonry structure. In the façade, the Romanesque influence can be seen in the lower part, while the upper arches and crowning statues are Gothic.

Pages 180-181
Venice, St. Mark's, detail of
the façade

Page 182
Venice, St. Mark's, four
bronze horses which decorate
the façade

The gilded bronze horses,
pride of the basilica, are over
six feet high. They are a
Byzantine work dating from
the fourth century; along with
many other relics and precious
objects, enamels and icons,
they represent the treasure of
St. Mark's. These works are
all rich booty of the Fourth
Crusade, which was led by the
Venetian Republic and ended
in the sack of Constantinople.

Page 183
Venice, St. Mark's, interior

The interior of the basilica is
of incredible richness. Mosaics
entirely cover the upper part
of the building; precious
multi-colored marble and
ancient and medieval columns
can be found. Here, with the
golden light flooding this
basilica, it is clear why
Emperor Basil II referred to
Venice as "Beloved daughter
of Byzantium."

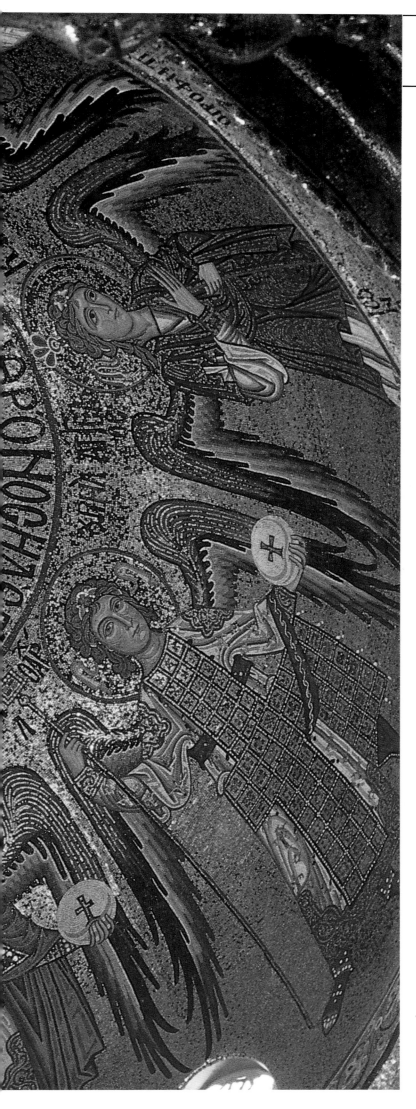

REMEMBERING THE NORMAN KINGS

Arab-Norman Palermo is represented in all its splendor by the Cappella Palatina, the royal oratory built by Roger II in the Palazzo dei Normanni, an extraordinary example of different moods coexisting in a single building. The small basilica has three apses and three naves divided by columns which are supported

by Arab arches. The extremely rich mosaic decoration combines the Byzantine and Arab worlds. The mosaics completely cover the walls, domes, and apses and are the work of craftsmen brought from Byzantium. The rich wooden ceiling with its decoration in the central nave is a masterpiece of Arab craftsmanship.

Pages 184-185 Palermo, Cappella Palatina, 1132 A.D.

Pages 186-187
*Monreale, cathedral, twelfth
century, detail of the capitals,
the apse, the choir, and the
bronze door by Bonanno
Pisano*

*On ascending to the throne,
William II wanted to follow
his ancestor Roger by building
a cathedral worthy of the royal
Norman tradition. This was
the inspiration for the
construction at Monreale of a
cathedral based on the one in
Cefalù. In this work, the
characteristic Norman
eclecticism is apparent
in works including mosaics
and fired polychromatic*
*enamels. Along with those in
Venice, the mosaics in
Monreale are the most
important document of
Byzantine mosaic art in Italy.
The church is also decorated
with two bronze doors of
western manufacture. The
door in the façade, inserted in
a portal with marble
decorations, is the work of
Bonanno Pisano and dates
from 1186 A.D.*

186

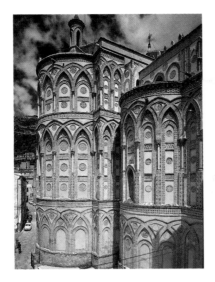

Page 188
Parma, interior of the baptistery, end of the twelfth century

Page 189
Benedetto Antelami, Descent from the Cross, 1178 A.D., marble, Parma Cathedral

The octagonal baptistery is the most important in north Italy. Begun at the end of the twelfth century and not finished until 130 years later, Benedetto Antelami worked on it as both sculptor and architect.

He was the first artist to change from the traditional Romanesque equilibrium to the new Gothic style, combining the tradition of Lombardy, his home, with his direct experience of French culture.

The primitive basilica of Sant'
Ambrogio was built in the
fourth century. In conformity
with the design of paleo-
Christian buildings, it had a
longitudinal plan. Over the
centuries its structure
underwent many complex
changes, finally culminating
in the twelfth century with the
construction of the present
basilica. This building is a
testament to the difficult
technical progress which
accompanied its
transformation into a
Romanesque cathedral.

Pages 192-193
Vercelli, Sant' Andrea,
thirteenth century, lunette by
Benedetto Antelami and
interior

This basilica, built by
Benedetto Antelami, is a
typical example of Gothic-
Cistercian architecture despite
the Romanesque features on
its brick and green stone front.
The central portal has a
lunette sculpted by Antelami
himself which shows the
martyrdom of Saint Andrew.

Pages 194-195
Vercelli, Sant' Andrea, view
of the vaulted ceiling

RELIGIOUS
STORIES

Page 196
*Assisi, San Francesco,
thirteenth century*

Page 197
*Assisi, San Francesco, interio
with frescoes by Giotto*

This church, the center of the Franciscan order, is organized as two halls with single naves and vaulted ceilings.
The lower hall functions as a large, dark crypt while the luminous, slender upper hall was designed for preaching.
This building is one of the best examples in central Italy of the movement from Romanesque forms to the freer interpretation of Gothic forms. On the one hand there is the austere façade and the sturdy bell tower; on the other there is the portal with twin openings, flying buttresses, and ogee windows.
In the interior, the life of the

saint is illustrated in the stained glass windows, which are among the oldest and most remarkable in Italy. The walls have frescoes by Giotto in the upper basilica and by Pietro Lorenzetti in the lower one.

Page 198 and following
*Assisi, San Francesco, detail
from Giotto's frescoes*

After 1296 A.D. Giotto began
the frescoes on the lower part
of the nave of San Francesco
at Assisi. These works
illustrate the life of St.
Francis, whose order was
expanding rapidly during this
period. The saint is
represented as an extremely
dignified man of his times, in
a clear break with traditional
ways of portraying saints.
Giotto shows the best-known
episodes in the saint's life,
while continually
emphasizing the reality of the
objects and animals and the
humanity of the people.
Moreover, in scenes (such as
the saint renouncing worldly
goods) the stories are set
against precise architectural
backgrounds and show
personalities who are real and
concrete both with regard to
their bodies and to their
clothes. In this way, Giotto
tried to bring the story of this
man who embraced poverty to
the new bourgeoisie and
mercantile reality of his time.

Pages 202-203
*Padua, Scrovegni Chapel,
beginning of the fourteenth
century, frescoes by Giotto*

*Giotto's paintings, done
between 1303 and 1310, cover
all the surfaces in this small
and simple private chapel of
Enrico degli Scrovegni. The
paintings define the space, not
only in single scenes but also
in the general organization of
the painted wall and the entire*

*room. The frescoes include the
story of the Virgin and Christ;
at the rear is a large scene of
the Day of Judgement, with a
portrait of Enrico degli
Scrovegni offering the Virgin
a model of the chapel.*

MIRACULOUS
PISA

Pages 204-205
*Pisa, baptistery, twelfth
through fourteenth centuries*

With its green lawns and
white marble, Piazza dei
Miracoli at Pisa is one of the
extraordinary monumental
complexes of Italy. It consists
of the round baptistery, the
Cathedral, the very famous
leaning bell tower, and the
large arcades of the cemetery.
The baptistery is built on a
Romanesque plan although its
final form is more Gothic.
Begun in the middle of the
twelfth century, it was not
completed until the end of the
fourteenth, therefore requiring
the work of many artists.
Nicola and Giovanni Pisano
are almost certainly among
the creators of the splendid
sculptures, placed in niches
that run around the building.

Giovanni Pisano participated in the construction of the cathedral at Siena, creating the beautiful façade. This is the only Italian example of this period of an organic relationship between sculpture and architecture. The statues seem almost to speak to one another through their interplay of attitudes and glances.

Pages 206-207
*Siena, cathedral, thirteenth
and fourteenth centuries*

Page 208
Duccio da Buoninsegna,
Maestà of the Madonna,
1311, panel, Siena, Museo
dell' Opera del Duomo

In the Museo dell' Opera del
Duomo (Cathedral) we find
this large work painted by
Duccio da Buoninsegna
(1308-1311) with The
Maestà of the Enthroned
Madonna with the Child *in
the midst of a group of angels
and saints. Among the saints
is the patron saint of Siena,
kneeling in the foreground.*

Page 209
Siena, cathedral, interior view

Page 210
Orvieto, cathedral, first half of the fourteenth century

Page 211
Orvieto, cathedral, view of the Chapel of San Brizio with frescoes by Luca Signorelli

The architect and sculptor Lorenzo Maitani designed the cathedral façade with the delicacy of a goldsmith. He used a wealth of spires and pinnacles, lace-like marble work, and mosaics. The sculptures are by Maitani, an artist who represented the most elegant Sienese taste.

Pages 212-213
Orvieto, Chapel of San Brizio, The Resurrection of the Flesh *from the cycle of frescoes by Luca Signorelli, 1499-1503*

Apocalyptic visions and terrible images are used by Signorelli to reject false prophecies and bring mankind closer to the Catholic faith. On the eve of the Lutheran reformation, the story of the Antichrist, the Day of Judgement, and the visions of Hell and Paradise in these frescoes reflected the tension of the times.

THE SUPREMACY
OF FLORENCE

Pages 214-215
Florence, Santa Croce, façade
and details, thirteenth through
sixteenth centuries

Begun in 1295 by Arnolfo di
Cambio for the Franciscan
Order, Santa Croce has three
naves with wide ogee arches.
In the middle of the sixteenth
century, Giorgio Vasari
modernized the interior,
removing the choir and
adding classical altars in the
side aisles. Among the many
masterpieces in this basilica, a
wooden crucifix by Donatello
deserves special mention.

Page 216
Donatello, crucifix, 1425,
carved wood, originally
polychrome, Florence, Santa
Croce

Page 217
Florence, Santa Croce, interior

Pages 218-219
Florence, Santa Maria
Novello, detail of the upper
part of the façade, tenth
century

Leon Battista Alberti, in
designing the façade of this
church, developed ideas which
proved extremely influential.
The geometric designs of
Romanesque origin are placed
within a rational classical
structure, combining the
traditions of medieval Tuscany
with those of ancient Rome.

Pages 220-221
Florence, baptistery and
Giotto's bell tower, eleventh
through fourteenth centuries

Dedicated to St. John, this
baptistery was built in a
Romanesque style in the
eleventh century on the site
of a building from ancient
times. It has the characteristic
octagonal structure and is
entirely faced with marble, in
a dramatic contrast between
the white marble of Carrara
and the green marble of Prato.
The interior of the dome is
covered in mosaics by
Venetian masters with
Byzantine educations. The
floor, with its bi-colored
marble insets, is decorated in
what can be considered an
Oriental style. The gilded and
bronzed door, made by
Lorenzo Ghiberti at the
beginning of the fifteenth
century, is rightfully famous.
It is divided into
compartments with Bible
stories and figures of apostles,
sibyls, and personalities of the
time. The baptistery also
contains a late work of
Donatello (1453-1455)
showing Mary Magdalene in
a distressing image of the
dissolution of a human being.

222

Pages 222-223
Milan, cathedral, fourteenth century and after

Gian Galeazzo Visconti, Lord of Milan, wanted his city to have a cathedral which would show the prestige of Milan both in Italy and north of the Alps.

The foundations of Milan's
cathedral were laid in 1386.
Its design, the result of
collaboration by many
architects (including
foreigners), came from long
theoretical discussions on both
technical and philosophical
matters. There were five
hundred years between the
time the cathedral was begun
and its completion;
nonetheless the architectural

*Pages 224-225
Milan, cathedral, windows
and two views of the interior*

style, based on northern
European Gothic models,
remained true to the original
ideas. The interior is divided
into five sloping naves covered
with groin vaults. The vertical
movement in which all the
architectural elements
combine is made more
evocative by the light that
shines through the splendid
windows.

TITANS
AND GIANTS

The program of Pope Sixtus IV for the decoration of the Vatican palaces was intended to celebrate the history of the papacy. At the same time, it was intended to merge the Christian vision with the stories of Moses and the life of Christ. During the first phase of the work, the best artists of the time were engaged, including Perugino, Luca Signorelli, Botticelli, Ghirlandaio, and Piero di Cosimo. In the years between 1481 and 1483, they created a plan filled with symbolic events and crowded with portraits of personalities of the period. This decorative plan was continued by Pope Julius II, with the story of Genesis painted on the ceiling by Michelangelo, and by Leo I, who celebrated the early years of the church with the tapestry cartoons by Raphael. Finally, Pope Paul III Farnese concluded this grandiose work with Michelangelo's Last Judgement, completed in 1541.

231

A THANKFUL OFFERING FROM VENICE

Built by the Venetian senate to thank the Madonna for her intervention in a plague outbreak in 1630, the Salute basilica was started in 1631. It was not consecrated until 1687. Architect Baldassar Longhena placed the grandiose dome on top of a high tambour circle, which in its turn is connected to the lower body of the church, making it one of the most notable features of the Venetian skyline. Using white stone, with a light gray covering the dome, Longhena fully exploited the play of light and reflection so typical of Venice. A similar play of light and shade is found in the interior of the octagonal structure; the load-bearing parts are of gray stone, and the walls are covered with white plaster.

Pages 232-233
Venice, Santa Maria della Salute, Baldassar Longhena, seventeenth century

Pages 234-235
Rome, St. Peter's Basilica,
sixteenth and seventeenth
centuries, overall view with
the square filled with people,
the dome, and the colonnade

In the reign of Pope Julius II
at the start of the sixteenth
century, the construction of
the most famous building in
Christianity began. Over the
centuries there were many
discussions about the plan and
whether to use the
conservative Latin cross or the
more innovative central plan;

the artists Giuliano da
Sangallo, Bramante, Raphael,
Antonio da Sangallo, Peruzzi,
and Michelangelo all worked
on the building. In 1547 the
job was given to
Michelangelo, who decided to
follow the central plan
originally suggested by
Bramante.

Pages 236-237
Rome, St. Peter's, three
different views of Bernini's
canopy

At the beginning of the
seventeenth century, a new
and conclusive phase in the
construction of the church
began under Gianlorenzo
Bernini, who was called by
Pope Urban VIII to finish the
work. We owe the canopy,
which was finished in 1633,
to him. It immediately became
the prototype for numerous
imitations and variations.
He was also responsible for the
large oval colonnade in the

square in front of the
cathedral. This solution is
skillful for more than one
reason. Not only can it hold
large numbers of people, it
also satisfied the Pope's desire
to symbolize the arms of the
church reaching out to the
faithful. The colonnade acts as
the solemn entrance to the
most important church in
Rome, and perhaps the world.

Pages 238-239
Rome, St. Peter's Square

Page 240
Orvieto, details of the
cathedral façade

Photo credits:

Antonio Attini - White Star
Pages 18-19, 20-21, 158, 161, 166, 196, 204, 205, 209, 210 right, 214, 215, 218-219, 240.

Nicola Grifoni
Pages 9, 46-47, 56-57, 84, 85, 87, 217.

I.G.D.A.
Pages 29, 30-31, 32, 45 top, 70-71, 80, 81, 86, 90, 91, 94,

Marcello Bertinetti - White Star
Pages 1, 12-13, 154, 170-171, 178-179, 180-181, 192, 193, 194-195, 232-233, 234, 235 top, 236, 237.

Giulio Veggi - White Star
Pages 184, 186, 187 bottom, 187 top right, 191, 207, 220-221, 222, 223, 224 left.

Giuliano Colliva
Page 188.

FMR
Endpapers, pages 2-3, 6-7, 10-11, 17, 22-23, 77, 78-79, 95, 118, 119, 120-121, 122-123, 126-127, 128, 129, 130-131, 138, 139, 169, 172, 173, 174-175, 189.

Cesare Gerolimetto
Pages 235 bottom, 238-239.

112, 113, 133, 136-137, 144-145, 183, 199, 208, 225.

K&B News
Pages 108-109, 148-149, 152-153, 206, 216, 224 right.

Nippon Tv
Pages 14-15, 226-227, 228-229.

SCALA
Pages 4-5, 8, 25, 26, 34, 35, 36-37, 38-39, 40, 41, 42, 43, 44, 45 bottom, 48-49, 50, 51, 52, 53, 54-55, 58, 59, 60-61, 62-63, 64-65, 66, 67, 68-69, 72, 73, 74-75, 76, 82-83, 88, 89, 92, 93, 96, 97, 98, 99, 100, 101, 102-103, 104-105, 106-107, 110-111, 114, 115, 116-117, 124, 125, 132, 134-135, 140, 141, 142-143, 146, 147, 150, 151, 156-157, 162, 164-165, 176-177, 182, 185, 187 top left, 190, 197, 198, 200-201, 202, 203, 210 left, 211, 212-213, 230-231.